COCKER SPANIELS

COCKER
SPANIELS

BARBARA ARNN

Photographs by Isabelle Français

Ariel Books

Andrews and McMeel

Kansas City

Photographs copyright © 1997 by Isabelle Français

ISBN: 0-8362-2644-5

Library of Congress Catalog Card Number: 96-85936

CONTENTS

INTRODUCTION

Cocker spaniels combine such a range of qualities they might seem to be the perfect companion for almost anyone. Merry and lively, yet attentive and sensitive; intelligent and inquisitive, yet tough and hardworking if necessary; cocker spaniels have proven themselves over the years to be remarkably adaptable to different environments and expectations. Although their history began in the hunting field, cocker spaniels fit comfortably into household routine; their eagerness to please makes them endearing companions. English poet Elizabeth Barrett Browning immortalized her cocker spaniel Flush in his role as comforter:

. . . thought on thought drew downward
  tear on tear,
When from the pillow, where wet-
  cheeked I lay,
A head as hairy as Faunus, thrust its way
Right sudden against my face,—
  two golden-clear
Great eyes astonished mine,—
  a drooping ear
Did flap me on either cheek to dry
  the spray!

Almost a century later, writer Virginia Woolf took this same poem as the inspiration for a witty biography of Flush.

This image of the cocker spaniel as an intimate, responsive friend has remained constant over the years. For instance, when then–vice president Richard Nixon needed to enlist the sympathies of his audience in an important speech, he chose his daughters' pet cocker spaniel, Checkers, as a strong, immediately recognizable image of wholesome, affectionate family life.

Your Cocker Spaniel

HISTORY OF THE BREED

The cocker spaniel of today is descended from a long line of English hunting dogs, referred to as spaniels, whose usefulness in the field and friendliness at home have made them favored companions to humans for centuries. As the English name suggests, spaniels seem to have come originally from Spain, as long ago as the fourteenth century. The poet Geoffrey

Chaucer mentioned them in 1368 (using the spelling "spaynel"). For the next several centuries, as spaniels developed in England, the same term was used to describe hunting dogs of several varieties and sizes. One type of spaniel excelled at retrieving waterfowl and came to be called the water spaniel. Large spaniels used for hunting game on land were known as field spaniels, and smaller spaniels were commonly known as cocking spaniels. These cocking (later changed to cocker) spaniels were used to locate or flush game from cover for larger coursing hounds to chase. Their name may have originally referred to their expertise at hunting woodcock. Some authorities have suggested, however, that cocker spaniels earned the name through an old use of the word "cocker" (meaning to pamper and indulge), and cocker spaniels may have been so called from the affection they inspired in their owners.

An 1805 description of cocker

spaniels says they were also called Sussex spaniels, so it seems that cockers were not yet clearly identified as a sepa-

rate breed. In fact, the same litter might produce both field spaniels and cocker spaniels, depending on the size of the pups. Later in the nineteenth century, the distinction became simpler: Field spaniels were those weighing twenty-eight pounds or more at maturity; cocker spaniels were those weighing less. Records show that some adult cocker spaniels weighed as little as eleven pounds.

By mid-century, however, these vague terms began to be used more precisely, and in the 1870s cocker spaniels emerged in England as a true breed with very specific physical characteristics.

Early cocker spaniels were longer than they were high at the shoulder, giving them the look of a tall dachshund rather than a modern spaniel. Black was the favored coat color. One dog in particular, Obo, who flourished in England in the 1880s, epitomized the type; his success as a stud dog reproduced his physical characteristics in a very high percentage of all later cocker spaniels.

At first, cocker spaniels were imported from England for breeding in the United States. One of Obo's offspring, Obo II, was responsible for passing on his famous sire's characteristics on this side

of the Atlantic. The English Kennel Club first listed cocker spaniels as a separate breed in 1892. After the founding of the American Spaniel Club in 1882, American breeders began to develop a cocker spaniel type with a more "cobby," or stockier, body; a rounder, more dome-shaped head; and a tendency toward longer feathering of the coat. Two spectacularly successful stud dogs, Red Brucie in the 1920s and Torohill Trader in the 1930s, are credited with helping to standardize the American cocker spaniel.

Throughout the 1930s both American-bred and English-bred cockers competed against each other in the showring and were commonly interbred, but nevertheless desire grew among breeders to have the two varieties recognized as separate breeds. In 1946 the American Kennel Club (AKC) did just

that, classifying the English cocker spaniel apart from the American cocker spaniel. Nowadays in the United States, the two breeds are known as cocker spaniel (meaning American) and English cocker spaniel.

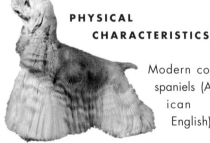

PHYSICAL CHARACTERISTICS

Modern cocker spaniels (American and English) still

share many impor-
tant physical traits.
Both are squarely
built and less
dachshundlike than
their nineteenth-
century ancestors.
The cocker's coat is

short on the head and furnished with the
long, wavy fur called feathering on the
ears, chest, abdomen, and legs. Both
types can have solid-color coats (black,
buff, chocolate, silver, or tan) or parti-colored coats (black and white; black, tan,
and white; or blue roan—a bluish shade

of black—and white).

The differences between American and English cockers are most clearly described in their respective breed standards. A breed standard is the official description of an ideal purebred dog, written by the members of a national dog club (the American Spaniel Club or the English Cocker Spaniel Club in the United States) for the purpose of maintaining the purity and health of the breed. Once the breed standard is approved by the American Kennel Club (AKC), each dog-show judge implements it by measuring each contestant dog against this abstract standard.

The AKC standards for American and English cocker spaniels classify both as sporting dogs and show the clearest differences in the categories of body size, shape of head, and coat. American cockers are smaller —fifteen inches maximum height at the shoulder for males, fourteen inches for females—than English cockers. American cockers have rounder skulls and a greater downward slope in their topline from shoulder to tail. The tail is docked in both breeds and should be carried in a straight line with the back. English cockers have a round rump, a more level topline, a longer skull, and less feathering, while American cockers are described as having pronounced spring and drive in their hindquarters.

The great appeal of the American cocker spaniel is heightened by his large, round eyes, with their soulful and intelligent gaze. These dogs have been bred to maximize the beauty of their coats. Indeed, the many successful long-haired show cockers of the last few decades have led some observers to suggest, not quite jokingly, that these "woolly" cockers should be considered a

separate breed. Different coat colors are usually associated with different textures, and parti-colored cockers in general seem to have less feathering. Long, wavy feathering requires a great deal of care from an owner, or even professional grooming, but the abundance of hair can also help cover or minimize otherwise visible faults in the ring. Breed standards in any case allow trimming of the coat "to enhance the dog's true lines."

BEHAVIORAL CHARACTERISTICS

As a hunting dog, the cocker spaniel's task was to run ahead of his human hunting partner, moving back and forth across the ground within gun range to flush any game in the area. When the game starts up, the cocker is supposed to stop and wait for the hunter to shoot, and then wait again for a command to retrieve any downed game or to continue flushing new game.

Cockers tend to run with their noses to the ground, but whether they trail silently or "give voice" appears to be an inherited rather than learned behavior. Treeing game is another innate ability of many cockers. Although most cocker spaniels now are household pets, not hunting dogs, they still take easily to

retrieving, even to retrieving in water. Their passionate interest in picking things up and carrying them around

(evidence of a strong instinctive drive) makes them excellent retrievers of slippers, golf balls, and newspapers.

Whether you train your cocker spaniel to hunt or to bring you the morning paper, or choose not to teach him any tricks at all, given the appropriate care and attention he will happily serve as a devoted, attentive, and uncritical companion from the time you first bring him home.

Your Cocker Spaniel Puppy

CHOOSING A PUPPY

How can you choose just one little cocker spaniel from a litter of beguiling puppies? In fact, two cockers can be excellent company for each other, and they can help socialize each other as well. But whether you want one or more than one cocker to share your life, you are looking for the same basic qualities: good health, good temper, and intelligence. There are no significant differences in temperament between male and female cockers, so the choice of sex is a

matter of personal preference. Whatever the role you want him to play in your life, your cocker spaniel puppy will respond eagerly to care, patience, and affection.

A reputable professional breeder is the source most likely to provide you with a healthy, well-socialized puppy. If you have decided you are looking for a pet and do not require a show dog, a kennel may be able to sell you a puppy that, though sound, is not quite up to competition requirements due to some minor physical deviation from the standard. If you are interested in training a cocker spaniel for field work, it is important to find a puppy who gives promise of being eager to work and able to concentrate well.

If at all possible, you should first visit a litter when the puppies are five or six weeks old. Eight weeks is considered the best age to separate puppies from their littermates (some states even have laws prohibiting the sale of puppies before the age of eight weeks). Observing a litter of puppies at play can give you important clues to their temperaments and personalities. A friendly puppy is probably a better choice than a shy one, no matter which type of cocker spaniel you have decided on.

A professional trainer or breeder should supply a formal purchase agreement for a purebred cocker spaniel puppy. The agreement will include the dog's sex, birth date, color, purchase price, and AKC registration numbers for its parents (you should also receive an AKC application so you can register your puppy). Some purchase agreements include conditions to the sale of the puppy or even its future use. The agreement may not allow any breeding of the dog at all, or the seller may retain all or some of the breeding rights. The buyer may be required to

agree to use the dog only for the intended purpose stated in the agreement, in competition, for instance. Some breeders will also supply a written guarantee that the puppy will not exhibit such common genetic problems as hip dysplasia or diseases of the eye.

PUPPY CARE

As does any breed, cocker spaniels require special care when they are young, especially as they make the transition from their first home to your home.

It's important to minimize the stress on your pup when he first arrives to live with you. You can do this by paying close attention to him, petting him, and talking to him. Introduce him to all the members of his new family, both human and ani-

mal (under supervision and preferably one at a time), and provide him with a safe but not an isolated place to rest. Such a place might be a wire crate supplied with bedding and a cover to keep out drafts. For the first few days your cocker puppy needs lots of extra attention. Leaving a puppy alone for any length of time will cause him to feel lonely, frightened, abandoned, or bored—all feelings that can lead to destructive behavior such as chewing.

Your puppy will need to be vaccinated with a series of shots, beginning some time between his eighth and twelfth week of age. These vaccinations are meant to protect your dog from distemper, hepatitis, leptospirosis, parvovirus, and rabies.

By the time it goes home with you, your cocker spaniel will be weaned. Since the first few days in its new home are a very stressful time for the puppy, obtaining a supply of the same food it is already used to is one way of reducing the number of changes the puppy has to make. Feeding smaller portions for a while may also reduce stomach upsets. You should avoid giving the puppy milk unless it has been used to milk in its diet,

and avoid giving it milk during the last feeding at night to help reduce the chance of diarrhea.

At first your puppy will need three to four meals a day, but you can reduce this to just three meals a day when he is about six months old. By the time he is twelve months old you can begin giving him two meals a day. Each meal should last between fifteen and twenty minutes. If your puppy is not eating all his food, you should try giving him less next time; do not let uneaten food sit out. Since a cocker's ears are especially long and floppy, a high-sided food bowl can help keep them from falling into the food.

The cheapest commercial kind of puppy food is all-in-one dry food. Cooking and mixing your own combination of dry food, meat, vegetables, and bone-

meal can be less expensive than straight commercial food, but providing the correct balance of nutrients and cooking the food can be complex and time-consuming. If your puppy is healthy, supplements to commercial foods are unnecessary and may even be dangerous to his long-term health. If you need help deciding how best to feed your cocker spaniel puppy, his breeder is a good source of information.

The feathering of a cocker spaniel's adult coat begins to grow in at about five months of age (in black cockers this may happen earlier). Unless

your cocker puppy is kept outdoors, shedding will probably be almost constant, though not severe. The longer your cocker's coat, the more frequently he will need grooming to prevent matting. The procedure will be much easier if you practice grooming your cocker spaniel puppy with a soft brush from the time he is eight or nine weeks old.

BONDING

The period between three to twelve weeks of age is crucial to your puppy's development. The first few weeks of this period are devoted to canine socialization, as the puppy learns valuable lessons from its mother and its littermates in how dogs should behave. During the next several weeks (somewhere between five and twelve weeks of age) the puppy will form permanent bonds to its pack or to its family, and this is the best period, usually in the eighth week, for the puppy to move into its new home.

A careful breeder or owner will have accustomed puppies to gentle handling early on. Owners who work during the day may find it challenging to provide the attention needed to raise a happy, curious cocker spaniel puppy. One way to ease your puppy's transition to his new home is to provide him with a stuffed animal or other toy to sleep with (rubbing it in the box where he slept with his mother and littermates, if you can, is

a good idea). A clock whose steady ticking mimics the heartbeats of other litter-

mates may also make your puppy feel more at home.

BASIC TRAINING

Teach your cocker puppy his name right away, and get in the habit of rewarding him with praise after any positive

response to a command or correction. To begin you may need to plan any training around the puppy's natural inclinations—calling it to you when you feed it and it is already eager to come, for instance.

Teaching your puppy that "No" means "Stop what you're doing right now" is a good place to begin manners training. Housebreaking your puppy requires special attention: setting aside a particular area outside for elimination, praising him for any success, and following a consistent training schedule. Giving your puppy water only after a meal may help regularize his schedule and make the training process easier for both of you. Nipping or "mouthing" should be discouraged from the beginning. Cockers have such a strong drive to retrieve objects that a supply of toys for your puppy to chew and carry around is a necessity.

More formal obedience training can begin when the puppy is about six months old. A basic goal is to get your cocker spaniel to follow verbal commands without being corrected by a leash and collar. A five-minute daily walk in the yard is a good way to begin lead-training your puppy. You can encourage your puppy by rewarding him with an activity he enjoys right after a training session. Enrolling him in a puppy socializing class may be particularly helpful in preparing him for a training class later.

Another important part of training for your cocker spaniel puppy is teaching him to lie on his side while being brushed. Grooming and cutting the coat

is such an important part of caring for a cocker spaniel that you need to practice with a puppy so he will be comfortable with the process when he is an adult. If you plan to show your puppy, you should accustom him to a collar and lead early on. Socializing your puppy by taking him outside and accustoming him to other people, animals, and such moving objects as cars and bicycles is also important.

FOOD

An adult cocker spaniel will eat a daily ration of up to fourteen ounces of dry food, fed in just one meal. Adding warm water to the dry food and letting it stand half an hour before feeding may help avoid bloat. Canned food and semimoist packets, which have a higher fat content and can lead to excess weight gain, should not account for more than a quarter of your cocker spaniel's food intake. This is especially important because cocker spaniels have a well-deserved

reputation for being greedy eaters. One way to avoid this problem is to take away your cocker's dish after twenty minutes, even if food remains. If you want to reward your cocker with a food treat, giving him small puppy biscuits is better than feeding him table scraps.

It is important to wash your dog's feeding dishes and bowls daily. Ceramic or stainless steel bowls and dishes are more durable and easier to keep clean than plastic ones. And even though you clear away leftover food, your cocker spaniel should always have clean water available.

TRAINING AND EXERCISE

Your energetic cocker spaniel will need a consistent exercise routine to keep healthy and happy. A half-hour walk each day will suffice, as will a vigorous session of ball-throwing. Keeping a supply

of old tennis balls on hand is a good way to reduce the chances of your cocker's chewing on more fragile objects, such as schoolbooks or shoes.

For such small, gentle animals, cockers are quite sturdy. They take very well to being kenneled outdoors, as long as the kennel provides adequate shelter from inclement weather. Even if your cocker is a dedicated house-dweller, a protected backyard run will give him important space to move and exercise. The minimum size for such a run is six by fifteen feet, with additional room for a house with sleeping box at one end.

Rewarding a cocker spaniel for a job well done is much more effective as a training basis than punishing it for failures. And because your cocker spaniel wants to please you, it will respond to your persistence. Speaking firmly, with neither shouting nor scolding, and then praising a dog's successes will yield the best results. The sort of formal obedience training provided by a professional dog trainer aims at producing a cocker spaniel who will obey specific commands instantly: *Sit, stay, heel, come,* and *down* are a minimum working vocabulary for a well-trained dog.

GROOMING

Cocker spaniels with heavy feathering— show dogs in particular—may require daily grooming to keep their coats healthy and free of matting. A wide-toothed comb is most efficient for this; whatever equipment you use needs a weekly washing. Long-haired cockers also need clip-ping every eight weeks or so, and a bath and trim every four to six weeks.

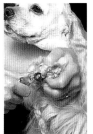

Grooming right before bathing simplifies coat care; some owners recommend using a conditioner as well as a special dog shampoo on your cocker's coat.

Every couple of weeks the grooming session should include checking and cleaning your dog's ears, always, of course, without probing, and no farther than you can see into the ear. Use a mild solution of hydrogen peroxide, rather than soap and water, to clean the ears.

Although exercise on rough ground or pavement should help keep your cocker spaniel's nails short, they may still need trimming from time to time. You can ask your veterinarian to show you how to trim your dog's nails (always with a special nail clipper). Keeping your cocker spaniel's teeth clean by rubbing them with gauze or a soft toothbrush dipped in a paste of half baking soda and half hydrogen peroxide will help prevent serious problems. Giving him a sturdy chew toy will help reduce the need to scrape his teeth, but any significant plaque buildup will require a visit to the vet for scaling.

HEALTH

Cocker spaniels have an average life expectancy of twelve or thirteen years, so you can look forward to a long and happy association.

An annual visit to the veterinarian for a physical exam to check for general health is an indispensable part of caring for your cocker spaniel. After its first series of shots a dog will need annual boosters, and the exam should always include a check for worms. In addition, the veterinarian will routinely check for possible abnormal conditions. At the age of twelve to fifteen months, your cocker spaniel should be X-rayed for signs of hip dysplasia, a potentially crippling deformation of the hip joints. English cocker spaniels in particular are sometimes subject to a degenerative, hereditary disease called late-onset progressive retinal atrophy, which may lead to blindness. If you decide to breed your cocker spaniel, careful investigation of his genetic background and health is crucial to success. If any tendency to hereditary disease is indicated, you should spay or neuter your dog to avoid the risk of passing on the condition.

Cocker spaniels need protection from the elements: a shelter and plenty of water if they are outside in the heat. Dogs who run outside, hunting dogs especially, are also susceptible to fleas, ticks, and mites. Once you have found them, the best way to get rid of them is probably by using a special powder or spray. In serious cases you may need to bathe your dog with an insecticidal shampoo and wash all its bedding as well.

THE SHOW CIRCUIT

A champion cocker spaniel is born with its outstanding physical conformation, but a successful cocker spaniel for show can be trained to excel in other qualities. He learns to ignore noise and crowds in the ring, to concentrate on his handler, to hold a pose, and to move around the ring in the proper gait. His training in these accomplishments begins when he is still a puppy. His owner will practice "stacking" him, or setting him up in a formal pose to show his best points, and will accustom him to handling by strangers. The entry of any purebred cocker on the show circuit is both the culmination of long training and the beginning of an arduous, but potentially exciting, contest.

The American Kennel Club was established in 1884, in part to establish rules for dog shows. There are currently more than five hundred member dog clubs in the AKC, which recognizes more than 130 registered breeds. The AKC does not have individual members, only group, or club memberships. The organization keeps Stud Book records of all dogs ever registered with it and adopts rules for shows, obedience trials, and herding tests.

Showing and judging the conformation of dogs is considered a sport: the dog sport. Each year in the United States there are over ten thousand competitive events—dog shows, field trials, obedience trials. The dog show, which emphasizes conformation, or how close competitors come to achieving the breed standard, is the most common kind of

show. Categories for entry in a given show can include Puppy (sometimes divided into two separate age classes of six to nine months and nine to twelve months), Novice, Bred-by-Exhibitor, American-Bred, and Open.

At licensed events, competitors win points toward titles. Overall winners of shows sponsored by individual breed clubs earn the title Best of Breed, and all-breed clubs sponsor shows lead-

ing to the title of Best in Show. Five points is the maximum a competitor can win in one show; a dog that has won fifteen points in AKC-licensed shows is an AKC champion.

The best known and most prestigious dog show in the United States is the annual event sponsored by the Westminster Kennel Club in New York. Every dog that enters Westminster is already a champion, and some exhibitors enter the competition simply for the honor of saying that their dogs participated in the Westminster show; the annual show book is a cherished keepsake.

The responsibility of a judge is heavy, and judges themselves are subject to strict requirements before they are accredited by the AKC. A judge is expected to have had at least ten years' dog-show experience before applying to be certified, must specify which breed (or breeds) he or she wishes to evaluate, must have owned or exhibited dogs of that breed, and must have bred at least four litters of the same breed. Furthermore, a candidate must have had five AKC stewarding assignments, pass a rules test and a test on breed standards, and supply references in order to be accredited.

It is the judges who determine the winners of a show, but a judge can only select the best dog in any category at that single event and on that single day. The knowledge that on a different day, and in a different field of competitors, the outcome might well be very different is part of the essence of the dog sport a source of its fascination and its drama.

The text of this book was set in
Futura Book, with Odeon
Condensed display type.

Book design by Jaye Zimet